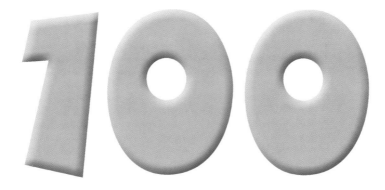

100

things you should know about

KINGS & QUEENS

100

things you should know about

KINGS & QUEENS

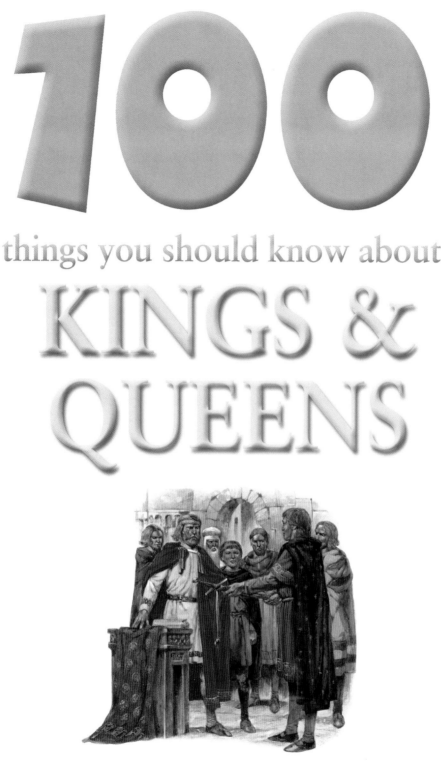

Fiona Macdonald

Consultant: Philip Steele

BARNES
&NOBLE
BOOKS
NEW YORK

First published in 2003 by
Miles Kelly Publishing Ltd
Bardfield Centre, Great Bardfield, Essex, CM7 4SL, U.K.

2 4 6 8 10 9 7 5 3 1

Publishing Director: Anne Marshall
Project Management: Belinda Gallagher
Editorial Assistant: Lisa Clayden
Designer: John Christopher, White Design
Copy Editor: Sarah Ridley
Proofreader: Margaret Berrill
Indexer: Jane Parker

Library of Congress Cataloging-in-Publication Data on
file at the Library of Congress

2004 Barnes & Noble Books

ISBN 0-7607-6098-5

Printed and bound in China

ACKNOWLEDGMENTS
The Publishers would like to thank the following artists who
have contributed to this book:

Steve Caldwell	Angus McBride
Peter Dennis	Kevin Maddison
Nicholas Forder	Maltings Partnership
Terry Gabbey	Alessandro Menchi
Luigi Galante	Peter Sarson
Terry Grose	Mike Saunders
Gary Hincks	Rob Sheffield
Sally Holmes	Rudi Vizi
Richard Hook	Mike White
John James	

Cartoons by Mark Davis at Mackerel

Contents

Rebel against Rome

1 **Queen Boudicca led a rebellion against Roman rule.** Boudicca was wife of Prasutagus, king of the Iceni—a Celtic tribe who lived in eastern England. After Prasutagus' death, the Romans took over his kingdom. Boudicca was furious so, in AD61, she led an army of Celtic tribes to attack Roman towns. After several Celtic successes, the Romans fought back and defeated the Celts. Rather than surrender, Boudicca took deadly poison and died. The Romans continued to rule most of Britain until AD410. Then the Roman armies marched away leaving Celtic kings and queens in control. We do not know much about them. In fact, the most famous Celtic ruler—King Arthur—may never have existed!

▶ Queen Boudicca and her troops destroyed London. During her rebellion over 70,000 people were killed.

The first English kings

2 King Alfred the Great ruled the Anglo–Saxon kingdom of Wessex from AD871 to 899. At that time, Wessex was being attacked by bands of Viking warriors led by King Guthrum. After several years, Alfred defeated the Vikings in AD878. Alfred then gave his attention to building new towns and churches and encouraging scholars. He was the very first English king to learn to read and write.

▲ This jeweled pointer was made for King Alfred and is decorated with his portrait. It was used to help follow lines of text on a page when reading.

3 King Offa ordered that a wall be built between his kingdom and Wales, to guard the border. King Offa, who ruled from AD757 to 796, was king of Mercia, in the English midlands. He is remembered for minting the first silver penny coins and for Offa's Dyke, much of which still stands today.

► This penny coin, made from real silver, is decorated with King Offa's portrait and his name.

4 Athelstan was the first king to rule all England. Until Athelstan's reign, AD924 to 939, England was split into many warring kingdoms. Athelstan took control of them all. Then he led the English to victory against the Vikings and the Scots in AD937.

5 **Ethelred gave away England's gold.** Ethelred II became king in AD978 when he was 12 years old, and died in 1016. Throughout his reign he had to defend England from the Vikings.

Hoping to buy peace, he gave Viking armies *danegeld*—large sums of gold and silver coins. But each year they came back for more. For making this foolish decision, Ethelred became known as "Ethelred the Unready" ("Ethelred-who-followed-bad-advice")!

6 **King Edward the Confessor became a Christian saint.** Edward ruled England from 1042 to 1066. His reign was peaceful but he meddled in international politics. To restore his reputation, his wife, Queen Emma, ordered that a book be written praising his life and devotion to God. When people read this, 100 years later, Edward was made a saint.

I DON'T BELIEVE IT!

Norman noblewomen sewed a tapestry 223 feet (68 meters) long, telling the story of the Battle of Hastings.

7 **King Harold lost his eye—and his kingdom!** Harold was the last Anglo-Saxon king of England, and ruled for just one year (1066). He led his army to Hastings, in Sussex, to fight the Normans— invaders from France. When Harold was shot in the eye by an arrow, his men surrendered and a new Norman king, William the Conqueror, came to power.

◀ After the Vikings invaded England, King Alfred and his soldiers hid in the Athelney Marshes, Somerset. In AD886 the Vikings agreed to a peace treaty, which meant that southwest England was ruled by the Anglo-Saxons.

▼ The death of King Harold (center) is shown on the famous Bayeux Tapestry.

Vikings—fighting for power

8 Cnut the Great was the most powerful Viking ruler. He was king of Denmark, Norway, and England from 1016 to 1035. Although he was a harsh ruler, Cnut claimed to be a good Christian. To prove it, he staged a strange event on an English beach. He walked down to the sea, then commanded the waves to obey him. When they did not, he said, "This proves that I am weak. Only God can control the sea."

◀ King Cnut claimed to be weak, but in fact he ruled a large empire. He used his power as king to bring peace, which lasted until he died.

9 Erik Bloodaxe was a murderer—and was murdered. When his father died, he killed both his brothers so he could become king of Norway. To escape punishment he fled to England, where he ruled the Viking kingdom of York in AD948, and again from AD952 to 954. But enemies there forced him to leave and murdered him as he tried to escape.

10 Sven Forkbeard ruled England for just five weeks. Sven was king of Denmark from AD998 to 1014. He led many Viking raids on Britain. Then in 1013 Sven invaded England, declared himself king, and forced the English royal family to flee to France. Just five weeks later he became ill and died.

11 **Sigurd the Stout had a magic flag.** Between AD985 and 1014, Sigurd ruled many Scottish islands. He had a flag with a picture of a raven on it. Sigurd believed that whoever carried this flag was sure of victory for his army—but would die himself. In 1014 Sigurd carried his flag at the Battle of Clontarf, while fighting to win more land. He died—and his army lost the battle.

12 **Thorfinn the Mighty —Viking and law-maker.** Thorfinn was ruler of the Orkney Islands, off the north coast of Scotland, from 1020 to 1065. Since 900, the islands had been under Viking control. But this did not stop Scottish tribes from attacking. Thorfinn defended the islands and then spent the rest of his reign planning new ways in which to reign and making new laws.

◄ After Sigurd the Stout lost the Battle of Clontarf, Viking power in Ireland began to decline.

13 **Viking king Sihtric Silkbeard was a warlord who wanted peace.** He ruled Dublin, in Ireland, from AD989 to 1036, but his lands were often attacked by Irish kings. To make peace, Sihtric married one of their daughters. Later, he gave up the kingship and went on two pilgrimages to the holy city of Rome. Unfortunately, he was murdered on his return journey in 1042.

New nations

14 Niall of the Nine Hostages was a pirate chief. Niall Noigiallach ruled the Irish kingdom of Tara from AD445 to 452. He made many pirate raids along the west coast of Britain, to seize slaves and plunder. Legends say that Niall was the first high king of Ireland, and the ancestor of the powerful O'Neill family, who ruled Ireland for hundreds of years.

▶ Pirate ships had shallow hulls so that raiders could land easily on rocky shores.

15 BrianBorú fought to drive Viking invaders away. King of Munster in Ireland from AD976 to 1014, and also Ireland's high king, Brian won many victories. The most important was at Dublin in AD999, when Brian drove Viking settlers out of the city. But Vikings returned and befriended Brian's Irish enemies. He was killed in the fighting that followed.

16 Rhodri Mawr (the Great) ruled Gwynedd, in north Wales, from AD844 to 878. He fought to defend his kingdom and win land, riches, and power. Rhodri also expanded his kingdom by marrying Princess Angharad, daughter of the ruler of the Welsh kingdom of Ceredigion. He took over her father's lands and became the first king to rule almost all of Wales.

I DON'T BELIEVE IT!

In 1165 Malcolm IV of Scotland (reigned 1153 to 1165) died because he went without food to show devotion to God.

17 No one knows where Cinead (Kenneth) MacAlpine came from. But he soon became famous throughout Scotland for his brave—but bloodthirsty—fighting skills. At that time the Scots and Picts ruled two separate kingdoms in Scotland. Cinead conquered both and became the first king of Scotland, from AD840 to 858.

▲ Viking soldiers probably helped Cinead MacAlpine to become king of Scotland.

18 People remember Macbeth as the murderous, haunted hero of a play written by William Shakespeare. But Macbeth was a real king who ruled Scotland from 1040 to 1057. Macbeth's life was certainly violent. To win power, he burned his chief rival alive, married his widow, then fought and killed another Scottish noble who wanted to be king. Once in power, Macbeth ruled wisely, defending Scotland from invasions and protecting the Church.

English – keep out!

19 **Llywelyn the Great demanded loyalty.** Prince of Gwynedd (North Wales) from 1194 to 1240, Llywelyn created a government to unite Wales and introduced new ways of ruling. He also gave orders for traditional laws to be gathered and written down and collected taxes in money—instead of in cattle or corn!

▲ Llywelyn the Great fought against rival princes and forced them to swear loyalty to him and his son.

20 **Llywelyn ap Gruffudd (the Last) was prince of Wales from 1246 to 1282.** His reign began gloriously, as he led the Welsh to fight against English invaders. But it ended in disaster. English king Edward I sent soldiers to kill Llywelyn. They cut off his head and took it to London where it was crowned with ivy and put on a spiked pole. Llywelyn was the last Welsh prince to rule Wales.

◄ While planning his next battle against King Edward, Llywelyn ap Gruffudd was killed by English soldiers.

21

One king's protector turned into his ruler. From 1132 to 1166, Dairmait Mac Murchadha (Dermot Mac Murrough) was king of Leinster, in Ireland. Then his enemies chased him to England, where he sought refuge with Henry II. Dermot returned to Ireland in 1169 and Henry sent soldiers to protect his kingdom. At first Dermot welcomed them, but they soon took over his lands. For the next 800 years, and more, English kings claimed the right to rule Ireland.

▶ Robert Bruce became one of Scotland's national heroes, along with other fighters for independence, such as "Braveheart" William Wallace (executed 1305).

22

Scottish nobleman Robert Bruce lived at a time when English kings were trying to conquer Scotland and Wales. The Scots crowned Bruce king in 1306. At first his armies were defeated, but he would not give in. A story tells how, while hiding in a cave, Bruce watched a spider making efforts to repair its web. This inspired him to go on fighting, and the English finally recognized Scotland's independence in 1328.

I DON'T BELIEVE IT!

James I of Scotland was murdered in a sewer. He was escaping enemies through a drainpipe but became stuck because he was too fat!

Kings of Scotland

23 Alexander III (ruled 1249 to 1286) was a successful king, winning new lands and allies for Scotland. But he had no son to rule after him, so he married a young wife. He was so eager to see her one night that he set out on horseback. But his horse tripped in the dark and the king fell over a cliff and was killed.

24 James II was killed by his own gun. James (ruled 1437 to 1460) was interested in the latest battle technology. Unfortunately he was killed by one of his own cannons, which exploded while he was watching it being fired.

25

The tough ruler of Scotland from 1460 to 1488, James III made many enemies. One lord kidnapped him, another locked him in prison, and his own son helped plan the plot that finally killed him. James was stabbed to death as he slept in a cottage, where he was sheltering after a battle.

▼ James IV and leading Scottish nobles were killed by the English army at the Battle of Flodden in 1513.

26

James IV was a soldier, scholar, and sportsman. He ruled from 1488 to 1513 and won fame as a fighter. He was also intelligent, sensible, and fond of sport ,(especially jousting). James built palaces, helped schools and universities, and licensed Scotland's first printing press. He died at the Battle of Flodden, a defeat that marked the end of Scotland's power as an independent country.

James IV

MAKE SOME FLAGS

Try making these English and Scottish flags

You will need:

scissors an old sheet pencil fabric paint sticks tape

1. Cut out a rectangle of cloth from the sheet.

2. In pencil mark out your chosen design.

3. Use fabric paint to color the flags, like the designs below.

4. Attach the flags to the sticks with tape.

Scotland

England

Norman conquerors

27 **William the Conqueror changed England's laws—and the English language!** William was king of England from 1066 to 1087. Born in France, he became Duke of Normandy at the age of eight. When Edward the Confessor died, William claimed the English throne. He invaded, and killed king Harold at the Battle of Hastings in 1066. William ordered a survey (the Domesday Book) of the land so he could tax it. He introduced French laws and many words such as "baby" and "robe."

28 **William the Conqueror brought castles to Britain by sea.** His soldiers made them in sections, from wood, before they invaded in 1066 and loaded them on to their warships. When the Normans arrived in England, they put the castles together and used them as army bases.

29 **Was William II shot by a friend or an enemy?** The second son of William the Conqueror, William Rufus, ruled England from 1087 to 1100. He died, shot by an arrow, while hunting. No one knows who fired the lethal shot.

30 Henry I, the third son of William the Conqueror, was well educated. He is only the second English king whom we know for certain could read and write. He became king in 1100 but had to fight his brothers to keep power. Henry won, and ruled for 35 years.

31 Henry I left no son to rule after him. When Henry died in 1135, Stephen, his nephew, claimed the right to be king. But Henry's daughter, Matilda, was furious. Henry had promised that she would be queen. In 1141 Matilda raised an army to fight Stephen. Although Stephen won he was forced to agree to Matilda's eldest son becoming king after him.

▲ The Normans built simple "motte and bailey" castles. Each had a wooden tower, standing on a tall soil mound called a "motte," in Norman French, surrounded by a strong wooden fence called a "bailey."

I DON'T BELIEVE IT!

Henry I died from eating too many eels!

32 Empress Matilda was the daughter of Henry I—and she was as fierce as her father. Matilda was brave, too. After she was captured in the war against Stephen, she escaped from Oxford Castle through thick snowdrifts, disguised in a white cloak.

Quarrelsome kings

33 Henry II was strong and determined. Between 1154 and 1189 he passed many strict new laws. But he could not make his wife, the French princess Eleanor of Aquitaine, obey him. In 1173 she led a rebellion against him because of the way he was ruling her family's lands in France. Henry imprisoned her for life.

34 For years, Henry II relied on his friend, Thomas Becket, to help him rule. In 1162 Henry made Becket the Archbishop of Canterbury. He hoped that Becket would help him in his quarrels with Church leaders in Rome. But Becket took the Church's side. In a temper, Henry shouted out, "Who will rid me of this troublesome priest?" Knights rushed to Canterbury and killed Becket as he prayed.

35 Richard the Lionheart was a famous warrior. He ruled from 1189 to 1199. Richard was a brave fighter, winning battles in the Crusades (wars against Muslims in the Middle East), and France. But like a lion he could also be savage. After capturing the French town of Acre, he ordered that all of its citizens be killed.

I DON'T BELIEVE IT!

When crossing the Wash in East Anglia, King John I carelessly lost the crown jewels in the mud.

▲ Richard I was as brave as a lion—and his enemies said he ate his prisoners!

37

Henry III was England's longest-reigning king. After coming to the throne in 1216 Henry ruled for 56 years, until 1272. But Henry's reign was not popular. He made people poor by collecting taxes to pay for wars in France. Yet his armies lost most of the battles.

▶ Henry III's beautiful tomb still survives and is admired by visitors at Westminster Abbey today.

38

Henry III was devoted to his family—and to his pets. He owned Britain's first zoo. Henry spent the last years of his reign planning a new cathedral (Westminster Abbey in London), where he was buried in a beautiful tomb.

▼ Nobles forced King John to sign Magna Carta. It stated that even kings had to obey the law.

36

King John I was an unpopular ruler. During his reign (1199 to 1216) he faced many problems. In 1215, nobles angry with his rule forced him to issue Magna Carta. This document guaranteed people basic legal rights. But John refused to follow it and his reign ended in civil war.

Laws, wars and revolts

39 **Edward I tried to make his kingdom bigger and better.** King of England from 1272 to 1307, Edward made many new laws. He also wanted to win new lands. By 1284 he had conquered Wales and built splendid castles there to control it. He never managed to conquer Scotland although he fought many battles against Scottish soldiers.

40 Edward I was England's tallest—and angriest—king! "Longshanks" (long-legs) Edward measured more than 6 foot 6 inches (two meters) tall, and was one of the tallest men in Britain. He was also one of the most hot-tempered. He once tore out his son's hair in a fury, and broke his daughter's coronet. In 1290 he quarreled with Jewish businessmen over money and religion and forced Jewish people to leave Britain.

I DON'T BELIEVE IT!

When Edward I was stabbed with a poisoned dagger, people say his wife saved him by sucking out the poison.

▼ Edward I's Welsh castles were designed with strong "curtain" walls and tall look-out towers. Many were also surrounded by deep moats filled with water.

▶ Edward III's armies won victories against France at Crécy (1346) and Poitiers (1356). They were led by his eldest son, who was nicknamed the "Black Prince."

41 **Edward II married a "she-wolf"!** That's what he called his wife, Isabella. She was the daughter of the king of France. As king (he ruled from 1307 to 1327) Edward was foolish and cruel. By 1325, Isabella could stand no more and she ran away to France.

42 **Edward III claimed to be king of France.** Since 1066, kings of England had owned lands in France. Edward III (king of England and Wales from 1327 to 1377) also claimed he was the rightful French king. This led to the Hundred Years War between England and France.

43 **Edward III lived in terrible times.** In 1348 a disease called the Black Death, or the plague, reached England. Victims developed a cough, high fever, and black boils. Almost half the people in England died. At the time, no one knew what caused the Black Death. Today, we know that it was spread by rat fleas.

44 **Richard II was a teenage king.** He ruled from 1377 to 1399. At the age of 14 he faced attack from mobs of workers. They had marched on London to protest about taxes, low wages, and unfair laws. Bravely, Richard talked to the protesters and promised to help them—then his guards seized their leaders and killed them!

▶ Young Richard won praise for his bravery, but as he grew older he became proud and very unpopular.

The Henrys

45 **Henry IV was not the lawful heir to the throne.** After a career as a soldier, Henry was hungry for power. In 1399 his soldiers placed Richard II in prison, where he died and Henry became king. He killed many others who questioned his right to the throne. Then he developed a skin disease, which killed him in 1413. People said it was punishment from God.

ROYAL QUIZ
1. Which Henry beat the French at Agincourt?
2. Who died of a terrible skin disease?
3. Which king signed Magna Carta?
4. The Hundred Years War was fought between which countries?

Answers:
1. Henry V in 1415
2. Henry IV in 1413
3. John I in 1215
4. France and England

46 **Henry V could not wait to be king.** Henry ruled from 1413 to 1422. People said he was so eager to be king that he took the crown from his dying father's head and tried it on! But the king of France made fun of Henry's lack of experience. He sent him a present of tennis balls! This was his way of saying that Henry should stay at home and play, rather than try to be king.

47 **Henry V won a famous victory in the Hundred Years War.** In 1415 his army defeated the French knights at the Battle of Agincourt. Crowds welcomed Henry home as he rode through the streets of London, which were decorated with huge figures of heroes and giants.

◀ Henry V died aged 35 from a stomach illness caught in an army camp.

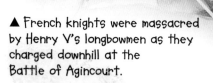

▲ French knights were massacred by Henry V's longbowmen as they charged downhill at the Battle of Agincourt.

48 Henry VI became king in 1421, aged just nine months old. As he grew up he was peaceful and religious but suffered from a mental illness. Without a strong king, rival nobles tried to seize power. During the fighting Henry's only son was killed and Henry was put in prison, where he died in 1471.

49 The battles fought between rival nobles during Henry VI's reign were known as the "Wars of the Roses." The nobles owed loyalty to two families—the Lancasters and the Yorks—who were enemies. Each family used a rose as a badge to identify its soldiers—the Lancaster rose was red and the York rose was white.

Killers and kidnappers

50 **Edward IV was a brave fighter, a clever army commander, and a good politician.** He became king in 1461. Edward liked food, drink, and pretty women. He was also ruthless in his search for power and gave orders for Henry VI to be murdered. When he suspected his brother of plotting against him, he ordered him to be drowned. Edward died in 1483.

► Edward IV won his first battle in 1416 when he was 18. Nobles fighting with him against Henry VI agreed he should be the next king.

51 **Edward IV's wife was no lady!** Few people dared disobey Edward—except Elizabeth Woodville. Edward wanted her to be his girlfriend but she refused. She insisted that he marry her, and to the royal family's horror, he agreed. Her family wanted to share in the king's riches.

▲ Elizabeth Woodville, Edward IV's queen, had five brothers and seven sisters—all greedy for wealth and power.

52 **Prince Edward was 13 when his father, Edward IV, died in 1483.** A few weeks later, Edward was kidnapped by his uncle, Richard of York, and locked in the Tower of London with his brother. The two "Princes in the Tower" were never seen in public again and their uncle became king as Richard III. People thought that Richard had murdered them. In 1674 the skeletons of two boys were found buried in the Tower. Possibly, they were the remains of the princes.

53 **Richard III was the last English king to die in battle.** Richard became king in 1483. Just two years after seizing power, he was killed at the Battle of Bosworth Field. He insisted on wearing his crown with his armor. This made him an easy target for enemy soldiers.

MAKE A ROYAL CROWN
You will need:

tape measure pencil gold or silver construction paper ruler scissors glue paintbrush scraps of colored paper

1. Use the tape measure to calculate the distance around your head.
2. Draw a crown shape in pencil on the back of the construction paper. Make the distance A to B slightly more than the distance around your head. Make the distance B to C 4 inches (10 centimeters).
3. Cut out the crown. Glue both ends together to make a circle. Leave to dry.
4. Decorate your crown with jewels cut from scraps of colored paper.

The distance B to C (4 inches/ 10 centimetres) is the height of the crown

The distance A to B is the distance measured around your head

54 **Richard III is a hero to some people today.** They believe that he was a good king and that the bad stories about him were invented by a historian, Sir Thomas More. He worked for the Tudors, who ruled after Richard.

◄ Richard III died at the Battle of Bosworth Field after ruling for just two years.

The Tudors

Henry VII

55 Henry VII founded a new ruling family. Henry Tudor was the son of a Welsh lord and an English noblewoman. He had a weak claim to be king but he won power by killing Richard III in battle in 1485. He brought peace to England, and an end to the Wars of the Roses. When he died in 1509, England was richer and calmer than it had been for hundreds of years.

1. Catherine of Aragon married Henry in 1509

2. Anne Boleyn married Henry in 1533 – she was beheaded in 1536

56 Henry VIII had six wives, but not at the same time! Henry ruled from 1509 to 1547 and lived happily with his first wife, Catherine of Aragon, for almost 20 years. But they didn't have a son and Henry was desperate for an heir. So he divorced Catherine in 1533 and married again—and again and again! Of the six wives Henry married, only one, Jane Seymour, gave him a son.

▶ As a young man, Henry VIII was fit, handsome, and liked music and sports. But as he became older he grew fat, unhealthy, and very grumpy.

57

Henry VIII led a religious revolution. He defended the Catholic Church against complaints from Protestant reformers. Then he found himself quarreling with the Catholic Church because it would not give him a divorce from his first wife. To get his divorce, Henry set up a break-away Church with himself as the head. It became known as the Church of England. Henry also shut down communities of monks and nuns who remained loyal to the Catholic Church —and took their money and lands for himself.

REMEMBERING RHYME

This rhyme helps you to remember the fate of Henry VIII's six wives:

divorced, beheaded, died, divorced, beheaded, survived

3. Jane Seymour married Henry in 1536 and died in 1537

4. Anne of Cleves married Henry in 1540 and was divorced just six months later

5. Catherine Howard married Henry in 1540—and was beheaded a year later

6. Catherine Parr married Henry in 1543—and survived her husband by one year

58

Henry VIII set up the first modern navy. He was the first king to realize that England, an island, needed a proper navy. So he paid for 20 new ships, all specially designed for war, and for full-time captains to command them. The most famous was the splendid *Mary Rose*, which sank as she left harbor in 1545.

▼ The *Mary Rose* sank after water poured though the gun-ports (holes for firing cannon) that had been cut into her hull.

Tudor tragedies

59 **Edward VI never had a chance to rule.** He became king in 1547 at the age of nine when his father, Henry VIII, died. But his uncles ran the country for him and did not want to hand over power. Then Edward became ill and died in 1553 aged just 16.

◀ Edward VI was a serious, clever boy who liked studying.

60 **Lady Jane Grey was queen for just nine days.** When Edward VI died in 1553, Jane's father-in-law, the Duke of Northumberland, wanted to run the country. So he tried to make Jane queen. But Mary Tudor had a better claim to the throne. Her supporters marched to London, imprisoned Jane, and executed the Duke. Jane was executed a few months later.

▲ Lady Jane Grey was beheaded to stop powerful people trying to make her queen for a second time.

Philip II

61 **Mary I was the first woman to rule England on her own.** She was Henry VIII's eldest child but the law said her younger brother Edward should rule before her—because he was a boy. After Edward died—and after Lady Jane was put in prison—Mary ruled England from 1553 to 1558. Mary was popular, but her husband, King Philip II of Spain, was not. Mary died without having children.

Mary I

▼ Many Tudor people believed that religion was worth dying for. Some people faced death rather than change their beliefs.

62

Mary I killed hundreds of people—because she thought it was the right thing to do. Mary was a devout Catholic. She thought that Protestant religious ideas were wicked and wrong and believed it was her duty to make England Catholic again. So she threatened to execute all Protestants who would not give up their beliefs—by burning them alive.

I DON'T BELIEVE IT!

Almost 300 people died for their faith during Mary Tudor's reign and she became known as Bloody Mary.

63 Soon after she came to power in 1558, Elizabeth I decided not to marry. This was partly because of her own experience—her mother had been executed by order of her father, Henry VIII. But it was also for political reasons. She did not want to share her power with any English nobleman or foreign prince. When Elizabeth died in 1603, the Tudor line came to an end.

64 Elizabeth claimed to have "the heart and stomach of a king." When England was attacked by the Spanish Armada (battle fleet) in 1588, Elizabeth rode on a white horse to meet troops waiting to fight the invaders. She made a rousing speech and said that she was not as strong as a king, but she was just as brave and determined.

65 Elizabeth had her own personal pirate. He was Sir Francis Drake, a brilliant sailor who was the first Englishman to sail around the world. But he also made many pirate attacks, especially on ships carrying valuables back to Spain. Elizabeth pretended not to know about them but secretly encouraged Drake—then demanded a share of his pirate loot when he returned home!

I DON'T BELIEVE IT!

Elizabeth I sent priests to prison for wearing the wrong clothes!

▲ Elizabeth knighted Drake in 1581 on board the *Golden Hind*.

66 Mary Queen of Scots became queen in 1542, at just six days old. She grew up in France and married the French king. When he died in 1561 she returned home. Mary was an unsuccessful queen—the Scots hated her—and a disastrous wife. She plotted to kill her second husband, Englishman Henry Darnley—then ran off with the man who murdered him! The Scots turned Mary off the throne in 1567 and her son, James VI, became king.

67 Mary Queen of Scots ran away to England and asked her cousin, Elizabeth I, to shelter her. Elizabeth did not trust Mary and put her in prison for almost 20 years. Even there, Mary did not stop plotting against Elizabeth. She made plans with Catholics in England and Europe who wanted her to be queen. Finally Elizabeth could stand no more and she had Mary executed in 1587.

▶ A Catholic plot was uncovered and Mary was accused of being involved. She was beheaded at Fotheringay Castle in February 1587.

When a king lost his head

68 **James VI and James I were the same man.** After Elizabeth I died, her distant cousin, James Stuart, became king of England and Wales. He was already king of Scotland, the sixth Scottish king called James, but the first in England with that name. He ruled each country separately – England and Scotland were not one united kingdom until 1707.

69 **James was the first anti–smoking campaigner.** Tobacco, which originated in America, was first brought to Europe in the late 16th century. It soon became popular but James hated it! He wrote a book describing smoking as "a custom loathsome to the eye, hateful to the nose, harmful to the brain, and dangerous to the lungs."

70 **James I was called "the wisest fool".** He was intelligent and ruled wisely, on the whole, from 1603 to 1625. But he did not look intelligent! His clothes were untidy and he slobbered and sniveled. He was also foolishly fond of several very silly friends.

71 **Charles I believed he had a divine right to rule.** King Charles (ruled 1625 to 1649) thought that kings were chosen by God. They had a divine (holy) right to lead armies and make laws. Anyone who disagreed with them was sinful. Not surprisingly, many of Charles's subjects did not share his views!

▶ A Cavalier (royalist) soldier (left) and a Roundhead soldier from Parliament's army.

▲ In 1653, Oliver Cromwell became Lord Protector. Here, Bible in hand, he makes a rousing speech to his Roundhead troops. Both sides in the English Civil War believed that they were fighting for God, and prayed that He would bring them victory.

72 **King Charles was a devoted husband and father and he was interested in the arts.** But he was not a very good king. He argued badly with Parliament about religion and taxes, provoking a Civil War between Roundheads (supporters of Parliament) and Cavaliers (supporters of royalty). After six years of fighting, from 1642 to 1648, Charles was put on trial, found guilty, and executed.

73 **For 11 years, England (and Scotland, and Wales) had no king.** At first, a Council of State ran the country. But in 1653 Parliament chose the commander of the Roundheads, Oliver Cromwell, to rule as Lord Protector. Cromwell was strict, solemn, and deeply religious. He tried to bring peace. After his death in 1658 his son Richard ruled—badly. Parliament decided it was time for another king.

I DON'T BELIEVE IT!

Oliver Cromwell asked for his portrait to be painted showing him exactly as he was—even if it wasn't very attractive!

A return to monarchy

74 **Charles II escaped to France when his father, Charles I, was killed.** In 1660, he came back to England to be crowned king. Many people welcomed him. Like them, he wanted peace and religious toleration at home. Charles II enjoyed art, music, dancing, and the theater— and he had many girlfriends.

▲ Witty, pleasure–loving Charles II was nicknamed "the merry monarch."

75 **Charles was interested in all the latest scientific ideas.** He set up a new Royal Observatory at Greenwich in south London, and appointed top astronomers to work there. Sadly, science killed him. His doctors gave him poisonous medicines and he died in 1685.

76 **Did James II try to pass off someone else's son as his own?** When Charles died, his brother James became king. But James wanted to make England Catholic again. He had a daughter who had been brought up as a Protestant. Suddenly, and surprisingly, in 1688 James announced that his queen had given birth to a boy who would be England's next Catholic king. People accused James of smuggling a baby into the queen's bedroom. Parliament acted quickly— and turned James off the throne in 1688.

ROYAL QUIZ
1. What did Charles II set up at Greenwich?
2. Who was king after Charles II?
3. Who was Mary II's husband?
4. How did William III die?

Answers:
1. The Royal Observatory
2. James II
3. William of Orange
4. He was thrown off his horse when it tripped on a molehill

77

Mary II was the daughter of King James II. Unlike him, she was a Protestant, along with her husband, Dutch prince William of Orange. After sending James II into exile, Parliament asked Mary to be queen. She agreed, so long as her husband could be king as William III. They were crowned as joint monarchs in 1689.

▶ In 1688, Mary II and her husband William were called back to Britain from the Netherlands to become king and queen.

▶ Queen Anne warned her ministers not to bully her into making decisions, just because she was a woman.

78

William III was killed by a mole! One morning in 1702, William's horse tripped over a molehill and the king was thrown off. He died a few days later. Supporters of James II were delighted and hoped that James' son, James Edward Stuart, would become king. They praised the mole which had dug the molehill, calling him "the little gentleman in black velvet."

79

Queen Anne united two kingdoms. Anne was the younger sister of Mary II. Her private life was tragic. She became pregnant 17 times, but all her babies were either born dead, or died very young. But her reign (1702 to 1714) saw major changes in Britain. Parliament passed laws uniting England and Scotland and banning anyone but a Protestant from being the British king or queen.

Rulers from Germany

80 **George I never learned English!** He preferred to speak German or French. He also preferred living in Germany, where he ruled Hanover and other states as well England. George was the great-grandson of King James VI and I. He had the best claim to rule England after Queen Anne died without leaving any heirs.

▲ This coin was made in memory of the coronation of George I in 1714.

▼ George I was king of England, Wales, and Scotland from 1714 to 1727.

81 **George I kept his wife in prison.** George's wife, Sophia Dorothea, was lonely. When she made friends with a handsome nobleman, George was furious. He locked Sophia away in a German castle and refused to tell his children what had happened to their mother. They never forgave him.

I DON'T BELIEVE IT!

George II died while visiting the closet (royal lavatory). He collapsed there from a heart attack.

82 **George II was the last English king to ride into battle—and he fell off his horse!** This happened in 1743 at the Battle of Dettingen. The British army won many victories during George's reign (1727 to 1760), conquering new lands in Canada and India and stopping rebellions in Scotland.

83

James Edward Stuart was the only surviving son of King James II. He lived in France, but claimed to be the rightful English and Scottish king. The British Parliament disagreed. They called James "the Old Pretender." In 1715 James invaded Scotland but he was forced out by George II's soldiers. He spent the rest of his life in Rome.

▲ Scottish highlanders, known as Jacobites, fought for James Edward Stuart and his son, Charlie.

84

Bonnie Prince Charlie was called "the Young Pretender." Charlie, who lived from 1720 to 1788, was the son of James Edward Stuart. He also claimed the right to be king. When he invaded Scotland in 1745 his attack went well. His army marched toward London but was forced to retreat by English soldiers. The next year, all that was left of Charlie's army was massacred at the Battle of Culloden, near Inverness.

▼ The Battle of Culloden in 1746 was the last major battle fought on British soil. Afterward, Bonnie Prince Charlie spent many months in hiding, until Jacobite heroine, Flora MacDonald helped him to escape.

The house of Hanover

85 **George III wanted to be a farmer.** George (ruled 1760 to 1820) lived during the Agricultural Revolution—a time when farmers were experimenting with new crops, techniques, and machinery. George was most interested in these new developments. He liked to get away from London to the country and talk to ordinary people.

▲ George III's long reign saw rebellions in America and Ireland, and a war with France.

86 **George III inherited a tragic disease.** In early life he was calm and sensible, but he had spells of mental illness throughout his last 60 years. While ill, he wore odd clothes, spoke to trees, mistook a pillow for his baby son, and believed that the baby was dead.

87 **George IV was regent, deputy king, from 1811 to 1820 while his father George III was ill.** George (ruled 1820 to 1830) did not take his royal duties seriously. He lived for pleasure—eating, drinking, meeting friends, and wearing the latest fashionable clothes.

▶ George IV was very interested in architecture and he paid for many fine new buildings, including the Royal Pavilion at Brighton.

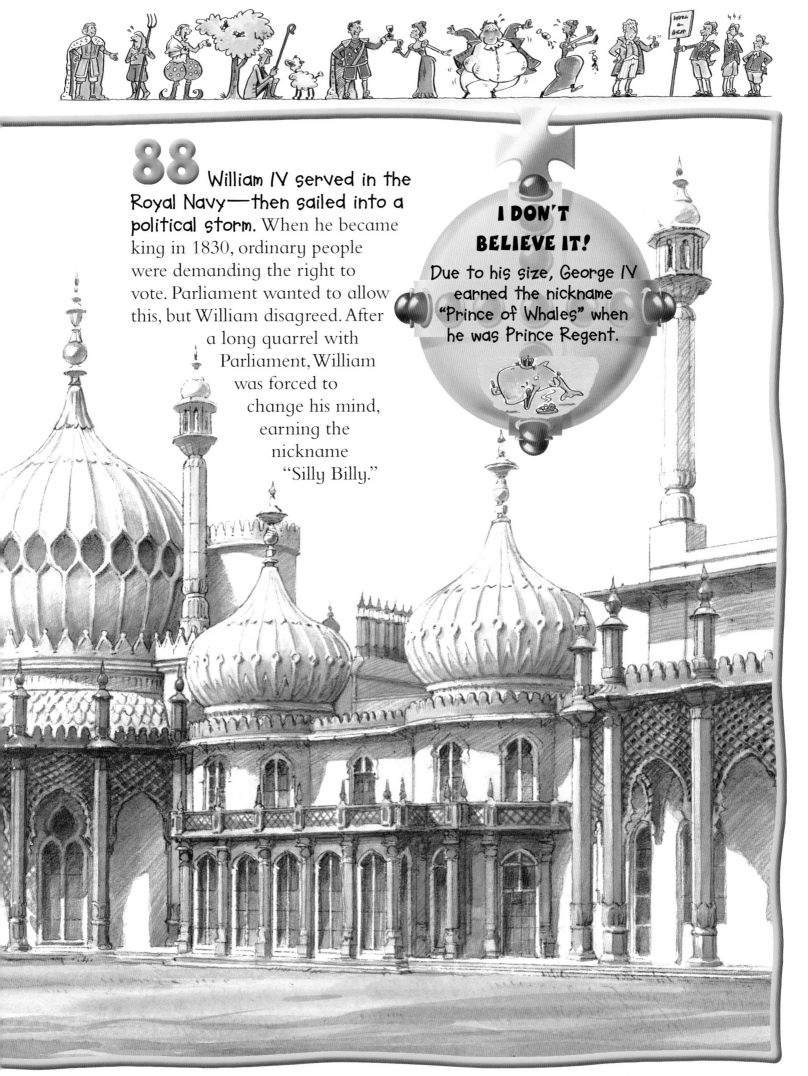

88

William IV served in the Royal Navy—then sailed into a political storm. When he became king in 1830, ordinary people were demanding the right to vote. Parliament wanted to allow this, but William disagreed. After a long quarrel with Parliament, William was forced to change his mind, earning the nickname "Silly Billy."

I DON'T BELIEVE IT!

Due to his size, George IV earned the nickname "Prince of Whales" when he was Prince Regent.

Victoria and Albert

89 When Victoria became queen in 1837, many British people hated the monarchy. They were shocked and disgusted by lazy, greedy kings like her uncle, George IV. Victoria promised to do better. She worked very hard at learning how to be queen, and took a keen interest in politics and the law for the whole of her life.

90 Queen Victoria became "the grandmother of Europe." In 1840 Victoria married her cousin, Prince Albert. They had nine children. Because Britain was so powerful, many other European countries wanted to show friendship. So they arranged marriages between Victoria's children and their own royal families. By the time Victoria died her descendants ruled in Germany, Russia, Sweden, Denmark, Spain, Greece, Romania, Yugoslavia—and Britain!

◄ Prince Albert always gave Queen Victoria wise advice, and encouraged British science, industry, and the arts.

91
Victoria's Britain was "the workshop of the world." British engineers and businessmen were world leaders in technology and manufacturing. They invented steam-powered machines to mass-produce goods in factories and steam-powered ships and locomotives to transport them round the world. In 1851 Prince Albert organized the Great Exhibition in London to display goods made in "the workshop of the world."

92
Victoria – "the Widow of Windsor" or "Mrs Brown?" Prince Albert died in 1861, aged 42. Victoria was grief-stricken. She dressed in black as a sign of mourning until she died in 1901. For many years, the only person who could comfort her was a Scottish servant, John Brown. Some people said that Victoria had fallen in love with her servant and they secretly called her "Mrs Brown".

▲ The Great Exhibition of 1851 was held in a revolutionary new building—the Crystal Palace—made of iron and glass.

93
Queen Victoria ruled the largest empire in the world. It included most of the Indian subcontinent. Like many other British people, Victoria became fascinated by India's cultural heritage and rich civilization. She collected Indian jewels and art treasures and hired an Indian servant to teach her one of India's languages, Hindi.

ROYAL QUIZ
1. Who did Queen Victoria marry in 1840?
2. What did Prince Albert organize in 1851?
3. How many children did Queen Victoria have?
4. Who was John Brown?

Answers:
1. Prince Albert, her cousin
2. The Great Exhibition
3. Nine 4. Queen Victoria's servant and friend

Into the modern age

94 **Edward VII waited 60 years before he became king.** He spent a lot of his time, while waiting, having fun—he liked sailing, horse racing, gambling, fast cars and pretty women. But he also had a serious side. He spoke foreign languages very well and was a skilled politician and diplomat. After his mother, Queen Victoria, died, Edward reigned from 1901 to 1910.

◀ George V made the first royal Christmas broadcast to the people of Britain in 1932.

95 **George V changed his name.** Ever since Queen Victoria married Prince Albert, the British royal family had a German surname, Saxe-Coburg-Gotha. But in 1914 Britain and Germany went to war. So King George (ruled 1910 to 1936) changed his name to "Windsor," the royal family's favorite home.

96 **Edward VIII said "something must be done!"** In the 1920s and 1930s, Britain faced an economic crisis. Thousands of people lost their jobs. Edward felt sorry for them, and he visited poor communities. He caused a political row when he gave money to unemployed workers' families, and when he said that "something must be done" by the government to help those out of work.

▲ St. Paul's Cathedral in London narrowly escaped bomb damage during World War II.

97

Edward VIII gave up his throne for love. He became king in 1936 and immediately ran into trouble. He wanted to marry a divorced woman, Wallis Simpson, but the government, and the rest of the royal family, would not agree. So Edward abdicated (gave up the throne). He married Mrs Simpson, and spent the rest of his life living overseas.

I DON'T BELIEVE IT!

George V had the best stamp collection in the world.

98

George VI never expected to be king. But after Edward VIII abdicated he was next in line to the throne. George ruled from 1936 to 1952. Shy and with a stammer, George found royal duties difficult. People admired his devotion to duty and his settled family life.

99

London was a dangerous place during World War II. It was attacked by German warplanes. Many Londoners moved to the country but George VI and Queen Elizabeth, his wife, stayed in London to support the people, even after Buckingham Palace was bombed.

Queen Elizabeth II

100 Elizabeth II has traveled farther than any other British monarch. After 1950, many lands once ruled by Britain declared that they wanted to be independent. Queen Elizabeth respected this, but encouraged former British lands to stay in touch with the monarchy, and each other, by belonging to a new organization, called the Commonwealth. As head of the Commonwealth Queen Elizabeth has traveled thousands of miles meeting other Commonwealth leaders and peoples.

▶ Elizabeth II celebrated her Golden Jubilee (50 years as queen) in 2002 with parties, free concerts, and a huge firework display.

Index

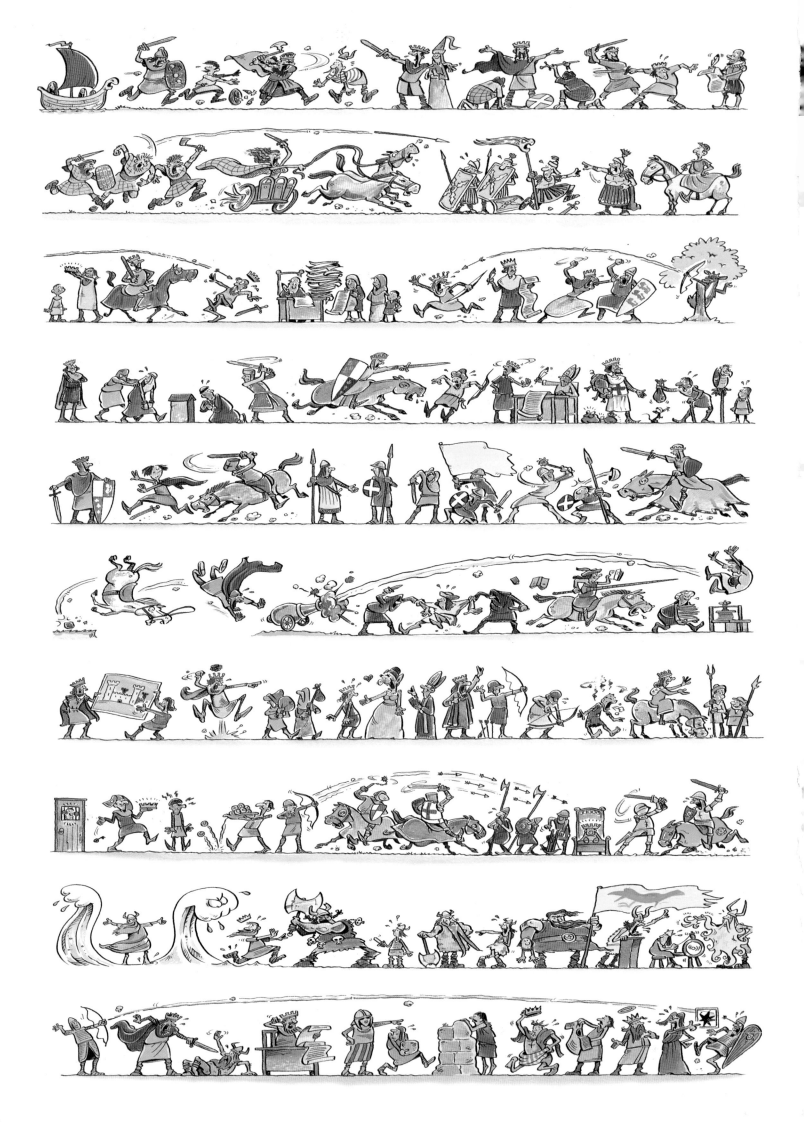